RELATIONSHIPS ON THE EDGE

HOW TO SURVIVE A CRISIS

STEPHANIE REGAN, M. SC. CLINICAL PSYCHOTHERAPY

CONTENTS

INTRODUCTION

> "When written in Chinese, the word *crisis* is composed of two characters—one represents danger, and the other represents opportunity.
>
> — John F. Kennedy

They say distance makes the heart grow fonder. But what if that's not an option?

Whether you're watching the news, checking email, or scrolling through social media, you can't get away from it: COVID-19, the ubiquitous, global pandemic of 2020. You try to stay calm, but there's a sickening anxiety rising in your stomach.

Maybe you're feeling trapped because before the pandemic led to social distancing measures, you'd already decided on some level that the relationship you've been in is over. Or you're living with someone who languishes on your sofa, watching you work while they binge-watch shows on Netflix, and you can only see arguments ahead for the foreseeable future. You're not sure how you'll manage it and how you'll survive.

Whether or not you already have relationship issues, the truth is it's easy to love someone when you're only with them for a few hours a day. But now, with sheltering in place due to COVID-19, we're expected to sleep, eat, work and play with our significant other every day without respite.

For some, this will feel like a jail sentence; for others, it's a workable challenge—an opportunity to have more time together and maybe to deepen and strengthen the relationship.

Perhaps you've Googled "how to survive isolation" or "how to live with your spouse on a desert island." But the current realities of lockdown, physical distancing, and everything else that comes with COVID-19 are new to everyone, so there's some potentially unreliable information out there. If you're feeling overwhelmed and unsure of what to think or where to find direction, this book is for you.

Maybe you've set up your new work-from-home desk right next to your partner's during this new lockdown honeymoon. She's been talking loudly on the phone all morning, seemingly unaware that you're also trying to be professional on a video call.

After she's done work, she says clients are dropping off, and she voices concerns about where money will come from and how the bills will get paid. Normally she'd go for a workout, but instead she pours a drink and flops on the sofa. You're left with taking the dog for a walk and getting dinner sorted. Perhaps in this scenario there are also children who now need home schooling.

At a minimum, you're doing your very best to keep those kids off their screens. You can practically hear their brains rotting from playing video games and watching that YouTube channel.

In normal times, you might press your partner to pull her weight, or you might go out with your friends so you can vent, but what do you do when your usual ways of coping are no longer available? If this is the question you've been asking, this book is for you too.

Thanks to COVID-19, life as we know it is forever changed. Everything that was certain and taken for granted is no more. Things we did automatically—like hugging and socialising—are no longer permitted. We can't distract ourselves with dinner out with friends, going to the movies, or picnics in the park. Social (physical) distancing, lockdowns, and quarantines have forced us to find entirely new ways to communicate, to maintain intimacy, and to solve conflicts.

No matter who's stuck with you at home or how you feel about them on a typical day, this unique time means conflict will be inevitable. But will it be the sort of conflict that forces you to address issues, find solutions, and build stronger bonds? Or will it be the kind that sends you and your partner to opposite ends of your home to seethe and brood in silence?

This book is for people who want their relationship to emerge from this pandemic (or any crisis) stronger and happier. Not just for a good Instagram story. Not just to make your Facebook friends think you're living a picture-perfect life. But as a genuine opportunity to deepen intimacy and appreciation for your significant other.

With some luck you will see new potential in each other, finding new strengths that you didn't know were there, and a depth in your relationship that you will cherish when you reflect on this period.

But how you react to the emergency itself also influences how well you'll get through it.

Understanding how you and your partner handle crises and stress can help you manage behaviours that you'll see during this time. Like a magnifying mirror, you'll view these actions in high relief, and they won't be easy to ignore. Is your partner the type who stress-cleans all your cupboards? Are they the sort who needs to hide under the covers and binge watch *Tiger King*? Or does it look like something else entirely? Whether or not you like it, you're about to find out.

***

The COVID-19 pandemic is a crisis of gigantic proportions, already taking hundreds of thousands of lives, causing enormous suffering, leaving loved ones to die alone and the bereaved to grieve without ceremony. As time goes on, we'll learn more about the virus and how best to test and treat it, ultimately protecting ourselves and our communities. Our public health systems will stabilise and prepare for the next emergency.

As we slowly and tentatively emerge from this season, we will hear individual stories, people's unique takes on this crisis, and learn about what helped them to get through. From the sharing of our collective stories, we will learn and adjust to a whole new world.

Like most people, you've encountered many challenges before COVID-19, and you've come through them successfully. Now is the time to remember these events and how you managed.

You may have experienced a serious illness or the death of a loved one, an accident, loss of employment, separation, or divorce. When you look back now, you'll remember that it took time to adjust to the situation. You needed space to recover from the initial shock, to accept the new reality, and to find a fresh way of going forward in your life, however much it had changed.

In the short term, a crisis puts pressure on us, often leaving us feeling overwhelmed and out of control. But in the long term, we face the future differently because of our experience.

While we had no control over the initial change, some seized the opportunity and made their lives better, stronger, and more resilient. You may ask why this happens, why some succeed where others do not. The answer to that question can be complicated and varied as each individual, each situation, is unique. In any case, your willingness to succeed, to grow, and to find solutions is a good foundation on which to build the resilience you seek in any crisis.

If you and I were working together in counselling sessions, I'd send you home after each session with a little homework. While the knowledge you gain during a session (or, in this case, by reading this book) is valuable, you need time to both digest it and to apply it. And so, you will see exercises—with clear rationales, corresponding methods, and results—in each of the following chapters to help you do just that.

Let's work together, in these pages, to explore the opportunities that our current global crisis can afford you. Know that whatever challenges you're experiencing in your current conditions and relationship can be a powerful means for profound breakthrough and unprecedented growth.

CHAPTER ONE:

WHAT IS THE CRISIS?

> "The struggle you're in today is developing the strength you
> need for tomorrow.
>
> —Robert Tew

Are you an introvert who's secretly thrilled for the excuse to stay home? Are you trying to make the best of the situation, exploring new hobbies, and finally weeding that darn garden? Are you baking a mountain of sourdough bread? Yes? That's great!

But I bet there's someone else you know—perhaps your partner—who isn't coping so well. You'll know that's the case if she cracks her first beer at 7 a.m. Or maybe she suddenly prefers the TV to even your most stimulating conversations, and you still have to love her. Or perhaps now that they have cancelled all the sports, she's obsessively tracking pandemic stats instead—and informing you about *every one of them.*

Living with a person who is not coping will put pressure on you. This makes you responsible for chores, for motivation, for setting the pace of the day, for all things physical, emotional, and mental. It's impossible to have a healthy relationship with a loved one who has switched right off.

First up: it's important to remember that we all react to crisis in phases. Initially, you'll feel shocked and won't quite believe what's happening. Then the reality will sink in. During the third phase you'll see what you need to do to make it through the event. Eventually you will have adjusted to the new order.

These four phases—shock, realisation, acknowledgement, and acceptance—are not necessarily sequential. And, typically, the bigger the event, the longer it will take to come through it or recover. The death of a spouse, for example, could take up to two years before the surviving partner can fully focus on their present life. But that's just a general observation, for the time will differ from person to person.

Let's look at some factors that inform people's responses during crises and stressful times:

DIFFERING RESPONSES AND METHODS FOR DEALING WITH STRESS

You've probably heard the expression, "The difference between stumbling blocks and stepping stones is how you use them."

If you think negatively about a situation, then you will feel the intensity of it more than others would. That's not to say that this pandemic is not stressful; on the stress meter of life, this could be a ten.

However, your ability to cope has a lot to do with what you worry about and how well you imagine you'll handle it—how in control you are.

Did you know that our bodies and brain chemistry respond to thoughts as if they are true? If you're fearing the worst, your body will react as if disaster is imminent. It's not just the crisis itself, but your fears about it that dictate your emotions, influencing your body and increasing your stress levels.

Perhaps you're not a worrier, while your partner frets about everything. Or maybe it's the other way around. People with difficult histories sometimes have a different "setting" for how they respond to stress—in particular, something that may trigger or upset one person immediately may not cause another person to blink an eye. So, it's important to remember that there's no gold medal for being the calmest person in the room during a crisis; everyone has their own strengths and shortcomings.

That said, the person with the most positive spin on a situation is more likely to respond with less damage to their well-being than the one who responds negatively.

PHYSICAL, MENTAL, AND EMOTIONAL WEAR AND TEAR BEFORE THE CRISIS

Because stress is cumulative and can build in your system, leaving you susceptible to a state of overload, what's happened in the previous six months is important. If your life was fairly free of stress before this crisis, you will probably fare better than someone whose world was falling apart.

Where do you and your partner fall on this stress continuum?

No matter what your life was like before now, this pandemic and lockdown is sufficiently intense that it will create a level of stress for everyone. It's okay to acknowledge that this is your first pandemic and that you're feeling way in over your head.

The strain of this can bring out some less attractive qualities in both of you. And yet, you and your significant other now need each other more than ever.

You can't change much of what's happening, but you *can* unload each other's burdens. Don't expect too much—allow for different reactions, and be kinder to yourself and your partner.

Prior experience with adversity and lessons learned

If you've had some rough times in your life, then I have good news for you: you already know how to cope with a crisis. Now you're tougher because of it, so you can afford to have compassion for others in your life.

But maybe your life has been *too* full of hard times. You've had hit after hit after hit—from a tough childhood to financial hardship to a few broken relationships. Bad things always seem to happen to you, or at least it feels that way. Yes, you're somewhat stronger for it, but you may also feel beaten down. If you've dealt with excessive amounts of adversity, this crisis can feel like a replay and just too much for you.

We *learn* from adversity, but we *survive* trauma. If unhealed trauma wounds are there, this current crisis may trigger you. Know this and give voice to it. Trying to keep this pressure under wraps will only make you tense and difficult to live with.

But it's also not okay to dump your emotions all over your partner. You've got to own your story. Talk through your feelings, but remember that they are yours to carry.

Positive attitude versus negative attitude

Are you a glass half full or glass half empty person? When challenges and obstacles arise, do you see solutions or just problems?

If you can find even tiny opportunities in this crisis, you'll get through it better than if you see this time as disempowering. You'll understand where and how you can take control. And your optimism for the future will keep you motivated to move forward with your life and goals. Even when you have setbacks, you will push through.

But what if taking a positive attitude is difficult for you? Research proves that while there is such a thing as negativity bias, it doesn't have to be a permanent behaviour. In fact, you can change your attitude over a ten-week period by practising "active gratefulness." This is sometimes called "cognitive restructuring." It's not necessarily easy to do, but it can be done, even if you don't feel like it at first.

EXERCISE ONE:
DEVELOP A HABIT OF GRATEFULNESS

RATIONALE

Adopting a habit of grateful thinking can help you feel more positive, happier, and healthier.

METHOD

- Take ten minutes to remember events that occurred in your day that make you feel grateful. They can be small things such as the laugh you had with a friend, the book you enjoyed, or the smell of the sea.

- Choose three of those positive events and remember as much as you can about them. Take yourself back to those moments and recall the pleasure you felt.

- Write the details. What happened? What did you notice? What are you grateful for when looking back on those moments?

- Make this exercise a daily habit if you can, but at the minimum aim to do it three times a week. Ideally, keep your writing in a single journal so you can refer to it whenever you like, and when you want and need to remind yourself of all the good things in your life.

- If you're doing this exercise as a couple, try exchanging lists. You'll learn more about what makes your partner happy, and you'll also have a chance to show how grateful you are for their presence.

Result

This habit will help you connect to nature, to other people, and to yourself. Over time, you'll find it easier to notice and value good experiences and appreciate the small pleasures and joys of life. This will give you the fuel you need to get through obstacles and crises of varying degrees without running on an empty tank.

CHAPTER TWO:

BEING ALONE TOGETHER

"Crisis forces commonality of purpose on one another.
—Michelle Dean

There's a real phenomenon that happens when you stare too closely at your face in the mirror. Suddenly your pores are huge, and you've got hair sprouting in all the wrong places. You start fixating on things you've never seen before; if it goes on too long, you convince yourself that you're unfit for public interactions. (Don't ask me how I know this.)

Anything and anyone scrutinised too closely for any length of time will seem flawed. So stop looking.

When humans first started cohabitating, they never intended it to be *all the time.* People spent significant periods of time apart. Hunting. Gathering. Exploring. Shopping. Doing stuff that happened out of the home and away from the person who was supposed to find them attractive.

It really doesn't matter how great a person is when you see him for a few hours at a time; after too much time together, he will become annoying. Even the American movie star Bradley Cooper makes disgusting noises, and if you spent a month sitting next to him you'd realise that he too does things you'd never believe a civilised, self-respecting person was capable of. "What's wrong with you, Bradley? Were you raised by wolves?" you'd ask. You'd call your best friend and complain. And your friend would agree that when you first started dating, they too had no idea Bradley could be such a jerk.

Now, with any luck, you've come across this book before the flaws of the human you live with have become unbearable. But if their habits are already starting to grind you down, the following suggestions will help you soften that reality:

Sync your schedules. This will be easier if both of you are working and keeping office hours, albeit from home. But if you're not, then creating a schedule—even if it's a very loose one—will help maintain a sense of rhythm that grounds you in time and space. Syncing your wake-up times and grounding your day with a joint activity like a shared meal will help both of you feel supported and connected. These mutual moments will help anchor your relationship and remind you that you actually like your mate.

Make a plan. It's important to sit down together and map out a strategy. If you're enjoying the lack of restrictions and conventions this crisis offers, keep your planning sessions light and enjoyable, focusing on goals and needs and how you might support each other. Use it as a time to identify potential issues and create agreed-upon solutions. Whether it is the towels on the bathroom floor, domination of the remote control, or the need to keep day-drinking to a minimum, you're setting down new rules of engagement.

Plan around obstacles. After identifying an issue, ask what conditions or supports you need to find a solution. Write down the solutions as actions. If you can focus on solving issues, creating this plan might be an opportunity to improve your relationship.

Write your plan down. Post it in a visible place. Refer to it often. Ideally, your blueprint will provide a positive reference point in your home by freeing up time and helping your relationship to thrive. You can adjust it anytime or even abandon it for a day or the weekend. But everything we know clinically and anecdotally from those who have managed long periods of unstructured time tells us that outlining how you'll use that time is key to keeping your routine—and your relationship—running as smoothly as possible.

To make your strategy a useful tool, consider these additional points:

Boundaries, boundaries, boundaries. The fastest way to make your partner detest you is to offer breaks or social chats when she's trying to be productive. How do you avoid this well-intentioned blunder? By having a productive conversation about boundaries! This might not feel like the most fun way to spend an evening, but nothing turns a person on more than being lovingly supported. So, start this conversation and watch her eyes well up with gratitude and appreciation.

Are you both working from home? Are there fixed hours? Who needs privacy and when? Who gets the office, and who has to work at the kitchen table?

Establish new boundaries that are above and beyond the physical. How can you avoid streaking from the bathroom while your mate tries to be professional on a video call? Can you come up with creative productivity bonuses? What are your rules around interruptions, lunches, coffee breaks? It's a good idea to understand how flexible these boundaries can be and how much concentration and uninterrupted time each of you require.

Rest and exercise to generate energy. When you're working from home, the line between work and downtime must be clear. Making time for rest and play is crucial. Therefore, if self-care isn't your thing, or if time off has never been a priority for your partner, this is your chance to either ask for help or offer it as a loving (but not too pushy) gesture.

For example, you may need to plan your daily walk/exercise into a certain time of the day. Maybe one of you will do yoga while the other cycles. What's important is that you both recognise what is crucial for each other and that you make space for those activities within the plan. Before now, you might not have considered time alone as a priority. But after living in close quarters for an extended period, you'll change your mind. Be certain to write this requirement into your plan too.

Resentment builds when people don't feel their needs are being met. So, address this openly. Be willing to pivot if life throws a curve ball. For example, let's say work runs over and you can't fit in your online yoga class before making dinner. If your plan recognises the importance of daily exercise, you can quickly sort out how to accommodate this need. No argument—dinner either waits, or someone else steps in. Everyone needs and gets their turn.

Playtime must be planned. It's easy to assume that good times naturally happen because we're together and because we're a couple. But if we're being honest, we must admit we know that's not how playtime works.

It's putting it lightly to say that as time goes on, it takes effort to continue to have nice moments and nights together. It's so easy during times of stress to transform from lover to (yikes) parent or (eek!) roommate. Your relationship doesn't have to go down like that, though.

You can suggest you share the planning for cooking and evening activities and that each of you will be responsible for a special night every week. If you can bring these apparently small things into your discussion and planning, then you both can take responsibility for bringing fun and enjoyment into your day and your relationship.

Feel like blaming? Put a pin in it. The very discussion of work, rest, and play brings important aspects of your relationship into view. It can remind you of issues you have been ignoring—and now you have the time to talk about them constructively, without argument or tears. Focus the conversation on ways to make your shared lives better and more harmonious. People are more willing to listen to feedback when it's delivered without emotion or blame.

That being said, don't be quiet because you imagine you'll rock the boat if you speak up and articulate your needs. Repressed resentment is one hundred percent guaranteed to blow up during a crisis. It'll probably turn into passive aggression—the single biggest killer of love, since no one can feel safe with or respect a martyr. It's not up to anyone to read your mind; it's up to you to articulate what you want and for your partner to respond. Just try to be kind in the way you do it.

Think about the way you want things to be. Imagine your days that way. Focus on future plans, not past errors. Inhale your future, exhale your past.

Exercise Two:
Know What You Want

Rationale

If you can communicate your thoughts and desires precisely to your partner, that'll go a long way towards having a harmonious relationship. To do that, you've got to be clear about what you want. These questions will help you gain that clarity.

Method

Grab a pad of paper and write your answers to the following questions.

1. What are my top three priorities during this time period?

2. What are the optimum times for me to focus on my work? Which times are written in stone, and which are more flexible?

3. What things would I rather do alone? (For example, reading, going for a walk, gardening.)

4. How much togetherness do I really want?

5. What are the signs I'm feeling crowded?

6. What am I worried or scared about?

Result

Putting words to your own needs and desires on paper is a good way to prepare for a conversation with your spouse. Your transparency will help the meeting stay calm and focused.

CHAPTER THREE:

WHEN THE PLAN ISN'T WORKING

" Coming together is the beginning. Keeping together is progress. Working together is success.

— Henry Ford

Every plan looks good on paper, but it may not work in real life. You can only judge the arrangement you've carefully put together by how effective it is for both people in the relationship.

Imagine this scenario: Somebody (not you, obviously!) is lying in bed every morning, hanging out in their ancient college sweatpants, with yesterday's chip crumbs still clinging to their days-unchanged t-shirt. They're not getting up to help with the kids or the housework, and you're feeling mighty resentful.

If this sounds too real, it's a sign you'll have to adjust the plan. Maybe wearing those sweatpants and lounging around in bed all morning will be a weekend-only event. However, unless your plan inspires you to work together, you'll soon run aground on much bigger issues.

If your arrangement isn't working the way you expected, it's time to rework your plan.

You made this deal because it set clear expectations and provided a direction towards a healthy, balanced home life that was an inspiration for both of you. Its creation was an opportunity for you to state your goals and voice your concerns. If you're not seeing the results you wanted, don't nag—just adjust the plan.

Think back to that earlier conversation: What were you wanting to achieve? (I hope you've kept notes, as now you may need to post them on the fridge.) Was there total buy-in, or did you sense some resistance? Now's the time to bring that up. Be careful about blaming or poking too hard; it may cause your spouse to shut down entirely. Think instead about what motivates them to step outside their comfort zone or what kinds of support they might need to stick with the plan (until it becomes a self-sustaining habit).

A PLAN REQUIRES BOTH COMMITMENT AND MOTIVATION

If you're the one who has noticed things aren't working as well as you had hoped, then unfortunately the job of broaching this topic will be yours. Start this difficult conversation now by asking, "Is this plan working for you?" You can let it slip that you're seeing some signs it isn't. But let your partner know you're a team and that it's in everyone's best interest to work together to get back on track.

When is the right time to have this conversation? My advice is to leave a little space between when you noticed the problem and raising the issue. How much space is "a little?" Hours at least or, in this context, a day at the most—just until any emotional charge is gone and you can focus on finding a solution.

A note of caution: what you see as a lack of commitment to a system could be more about your partner having difficulty staying motivated. Maybe she's dealing with her own depression and anxiety. Don't assume you understand what you're seeing. Be curious. Find out. Whatever you do, resist the urge to call her friends and complain. It's way too hard to come back from that.

It's also important to know that when we're under pressure we revert to patterns—to our old ways and old style (do you hear yourself channelling your mother?). If it's happening to him, it's probably happening to you too. Be aware and own it. You'll have much more credibility in this discussion if you take responsibility for your own imperfections before you launch into pointing out your partner's. Chances are good that one patterned behaviour ignites or feeds into the other.

Perhaps your mate just can't see the point in the arrangement that you both agreed to. If so, go back to the drawing board and have that discussion again.

AGREE THAT NEITHER OF YOU CAN OPT OUT OF THE PLAN

You must take responsibility for your own well-being; it's not okay to expect someone else to do it for you. So, take care of yourself, and insist that your spouse do the same. That's not to say you can't support and encourage each other—but don't let her mood drag you down. And she shouldn't expect you to nag her into compliance.

STAYING IN BED ALL DAY IS NOT A CHOICE

Unless you are ill or are a cat, hiding under the covers is not a solution or a viable option. You need structure in your life—and, lucky you, now you know how to create it because you have a plan!

The mantra of work, rest, and play applies every day. You may not be working for someone else, but you still need to be productive. When you get things done, you feel good, and it lifts the mood of everyone else in the house too. It's also what makes rest and play periods feel different and special rather than lost in a blur of endless time.

LITTLE THINGS MAKE BIG DAYS

When you don't have the obligation to go to work, to dress up, or impress others, you can end up in a slump. You can't find your motivation.

Highly motivated people often have very good habits. Like personal psychological hygiene, they wake with a small plan and get started on the day. Maybe for you it's harder to keep that plan in view when no one is pushing you forward; if so, you might need to look at that. Here are some great questions to get your planning back on track:

- How do you spend your day? What things do you do for others, for yourself, and for your partner? How long does it all take?

- Who in your life is important to you?

- What is it you want for yourself?

- What motivates you? If you can identify it, you can find creative ways to recreate those conditions. Is it praise? Little treats?

- Is there anything in the current plan that works for you? Anything you'd like to do differently? Adjust your plan to make these changes and ask for feedback along the way.

Asking these questions is also a great way to keep both you and your mate on track. Plus, it will give you something interesting to talk about at the end of each day.

If getting started is the biggest hurdle, pretend you've just received the following orders from someone you trust and respect:

Work: If you're working from home, then schedule at least one meeting for first thing each morning. If there's no work, then schedule an online coffee date—not at the crack of dawn, obviously, but early enough to motivate a healthy morning routine.

Choose your time to rise—7, 8 or 9 a.m. Shower, dress and be ready because this is the most industrious time of your day. You have the freedom to decide what you will do, but that time has to feel productive.

The more you do and the more you achieve, the better you will feel and the more motivated you will be for the next day.

Rest: Finding an activity that is restful, peaceful, and just for you alone is essential. You're cooped up 24/7 with your partner, responding to her needs, trying to show some interest in whatever she's talking about. And tomorrow may be no different. So, take some time for you—walk outdoors, spend time in your garden, read a book, or hide out in the bathtub.

Play: There are lots of fun things to do online during this time, from classes offered by celebrities to virtual dance parties to dinner gatherings on Zoom. But you won't find them unless you make the effort to look. Think beyond Facebook and Twitter and Instagram, which encourage passive scrolling rather than active participation. Once you've determined what fun things you'd like to take part in, see if your partner would like to do them with you. Here are a few ideas to get you started:

- Update your cooking skills! In fact, Ireland is now being hailed as the "banana bread republic" because of the country's exceptional fascination with this comforting treat.

- Run a quiz, karaoke, or charades night with friends over Zoom.

- Host a dinner party with a theme—wigs, mad hats, or wacky glasses nights.

- Take a virtual tour of the National Gallery:
  [https://www.nationalgallery.ie/virtual-tour]

- Catch a play on London's West End and bring the very best of theatre to your own sitting room:
  [https://www.nationaltheatre.org.uk/nt-at-home]

- See lots more ideas here:
  [https://www.futurelearn.com/info/blog/50-free-things-you-can-do-during-lockdown]

Anxiety

Maybe the plan isn't working, despite both of you feeling committed and motivated. Maybe the issues are deeper; for example, anxiety—clinical or situational—could be a factor.

I think we're all feeling apprehensive right now. Life as we know it has changed, and our future is uncertain. The images on our television screens are so deeply sad, and the loss that people are enduring is enormous.

However, some of us have a greater tendency towards anxiety, which can show up as forgetfulness, difficulty focusing, irritability, and anger. Maybe it's your spouse, maybe it's you, or perhaps both of you are feeling nervous and unsettled.

Thankfully, now you have time, space, and privacy to manage this. Consider that your anxiety is actually offering you some useful information. Often, trying to avoid or ignore anxiety only makes it worse. If you can talk it through or really examine it, you may understand what's causing it and then address it.

Ask your anxiety, "What are you trying to tell me?" and write whatever pops into your head, without editing or judging it. You may have to do this a few times to drill down to the source. But when you do, your suffering will offer its own solution. Working with your angst this way will increase your resilience and will make you feel much more capable. Unless your anxiety is primarily a product of brain chemistry, planning and action are often the very best solutions.

I often advise people with anxiety to limit their exposure to the news and especially to personal accounts of suffering, deaths, or situations with bad outcomes. Witnessing this level of detail is not good for you. It's fine to keep up to date with the news, but limit yourself to only the big picture stuff—what's important, new developments, and information that will help you to know if you need to modify your own behaviour.

Remember, too, that having structure, and committing to your daily tasks, allows you to focus and feel in control, both of which will help with your anxiety.

If you suffer from clinical anxiety, now more than ever is a good time to check in with your healthcare team; be sure that your medication, if you take any, is on hand, and that your wellness plan is being followed.

Some people find the H.A.L.T. acronym to be helpful—that is, check in throughout the day to see if you're **hungry**, **angry** (or **anxious**), **lonely**, or **tired** (or **thirsty**). It's said that more than a couple of these states at once will lead to overwhelm; using the acronym as an assessment tool can benefit anyone at any time.

Depression

If you've suffered with depression in the past, or if you are on medication presently, then you may find that this situation is more testing for you. It's a good idea to talk to your doctor, especially if you're feeling under pressure or you recognise symptoms that you've experienced before.

Even if you've never been depressed but now you're finding it difficult to sleep, or you're catastrophizing and seeing no future, these would be sound reasons to visit your doctor (even if it's by phone or online video consultation).

Much of what you see on television and online is depressing, so if you feel blue, it's no wonder. Many people can move beyond this and focus on their daily lives. But if you feel you're really struggling and that it's more than a mood that one can shake off, then please do not suffer alone—reach out for help.

EXCESSIVE DRINKING

Now that we're home all the time, there's the temptation to drink. After all, it's not like you're going to drive anywhere—why not have a few cold ones? And hey, it's okay if you spill that red wine on your sweatpants while you're watching TV at 8 a.m. Who is there to judge you? No one knows.

Numbing yourself with alcohol can make you feel great, initially. But there's a big downside. When the booze exits your system it leaves you even more depressed and more anxious, so what do you do? You drink more. And by the end of this pandemic you will have gained twenty pounds, some serious mental health issues, and a drinking problem. (We'll talk about this more in Chapter Nine.)

OVEREATING

It's nice to have a little treat every once in a while. Even a daily taste of chocolate is okay. But if you've just ordered the delivery of a huge box of half-price sweets, you may need to check yourself. You've gone from a "mood-lifting" treat to an over-the-top binge. Soon you'll be sitting on the sofa, hiding your treats, piling on the weight and hating yourself for it.

Just as in normal, non-pandemic times, you must carry responsibility for your own problems. I know that this may be difficult for you to manage alone, and it's perfectly okay to reach out for help. There is no better time to do that than today.

For help, support, advice, guidance, or to join a support group, you may want to consider Bodywhys, the Eating Disorders Association of Ireland [https://www.bodywhys.ie].

There are also some very useful apps, like Recovery Record and Rise Up + Recover; these allow you to log not only your meals and snacks but also your emotions. These can be found on both iTunes and Google Play.

EXERCISE THREE
LEARN TO SHOW APPRECIATION

RATIONALE

Your habit of gratefulness and a tendency to screen for the positives will make you a happier and healthier person. The same applies in relationships. It's easy to focus on each other's behaviour when something goes wrong, but it's more important to notice what works well.

METHOD

- Note three things that your mate has said or done that you liked.

- Let them know that you appreciate that behaviour.

  "I like it when you do _______."

  "I feel closer to you when _______."

  "I love when you _______."

Initially, you can do this exercise by yourself, but it's way more fun when you progress to doing it as a couple.

RESULT

Completing this exercise will foster the loving feelings that you have for each other as you will both feel more appreciated. It also promotes good practices, as you're both more likely to repeat whatever actions your partner praises. And when you're feeling more positive, connected, and motivated, it will be easier to be on the same page when it comes to creating and maintaining a shared plan.

CHAPTER FOUR:

MIND YOUR LANGUAGE

" Seek first to understand, then to be understood.
—Steven Covey

Are you the strong, silent type? The sort who pretends nothing has happened in hopes your partner will eventually give up and forget? That strategy won't work for you when you're in lockdown. And if your tendency is to be passive aggressive? Say goodbye to the days when you could hurl Jedi hate messages telepathically while slamming cups into the dishwasher. That simply won't fly now.

In the time before lockdown, your spouse may have put up with your aggressive communication style. After all, who doesn't love it when someone shouts a few insults as they storm out of the house before anyone can return the favour? There are all kinds of ways to avoid an uncomfortable conversation. But now it's time to make a hard choice: your emotional comfort zone or your relationship.

We've already established that you and your partner occasionally make each other nuts. Now it's time to turn minor irritations, or even more significant issues, into something more positive.

Learning to manage arguments and conflicts in a respectful, direct way will do more to deepen and blossom your relationship than even the most heartfelt apology. And the great news? Everyone can develop healthy communication styles. Here are some easy steps to take when communication has gone off the rails:

Choose to forgive yourself. You're not perfect. You may blame your parents for a lousy upbringing, or you may blame your ex-girlfriend who made you lose trust in human decency. But what it comes down to is this: *nobody* is perfect. So, now is the time for self-forgiveness. Choose to take responsibility for yourself and start over today, even if you don't feel like it. Fake it till you make it, as they say.

Announce your intention to practice healthy, direct communication. Tell your paramour you won't be great at it right off the bat, but that you're committed to the daily practice of it.

Ask your partner to practice with you. This way you're not taking all the blame or the responsibility. After all, communication is a two-way street.

Explain all the ways your partner will benefit from the two of you rocking good communication. And for goodness' sake, don't start your sentences with, "Do you know what your problem is?" Speaking of which…

Mind your language. The words you choose and how you express them are more important than you may think. Even though you're doing your best, the wrong words and tone may damage your relationship. Experts can predict the breakdown of a marriage by analysing the extent to which couples use "I" statements as against "you" statements. When you consider it, this makes perfect sense: when you use "I" statements you take responsibility for yourself, whereas "you" statements only blame your partner.

Consider the following two examples. Which do you think will elicit a more favourable response?

- "You never bother doing the wash-up."

- "I feel less loved when you leave everything to me. I'd like you to help me out."

The second example is better because it's an expression of your feelings and a request for help rather than an accusation or judgement.

An even more successful request might be: "Did you know that women find blokes especially attractive when they do the dishes and help around the house?" (For a humorous take on this, you may want to read the scandalously named but entirely harmless *Porn for Women* by Susan Anderson.)

Think about the statements you use the most. Take a moment to reword one or two in a way your spouse will find more appealing. Then reward yourself by drinking a cup of tea while you admire your lover's amazing washing-up skills.

DISAGREEMENTS

As I've said before: you will have disagreements during this crisis, but you don't have to let them take over your daily life.

Once the emotional heat of conflict has dissipated somewhat, raise the topic for discussion in a productive way by taking the following steps:

1. Acknowledge the facts.

2. Once you both agree about what happened (this is key), clarify your own feelings.

3. State what your needs are in the situation; make sure both parties get airtime on this.

4. Ask what your partner might require so they can meet your needs.

5. Make sure your partner understands that this is not about you giving orders for them to follow. This is about the two of you working together to ensure your requests meet the needs of both parties. Restating this intention will help you work towards a calm, solution-focused discussion.

6. Ask what your partner needs from *you* so you can meet *their* needs too.

You'll realise that you're making progress if you can discuss the issue in a manner that allows you to understand each other more deeply. Feeling understood in difficult situations is pretty exciting. In fact, successfully tackling disagreements can help your relationship grow, but this will never happen if either of you insists on winning. Talk less, listen more, and don't score points.

WHAT ARE YOU SAYING?

A happy person is much more agreeable than a peevish one. For this reason alone, it's in your best interest to make the person you love feel loved. If you focus your attention on understanding each other—finding out what's important to you and your spouse, what makes both of you feel excited, happy, and safe—then it becomes a lot easier to weather some difficulties. Hopefully it's not too challenging to show your appreciation and love in little ways here and there. At the very least, notice what he's doing and appreciate it out loud. Loving communication must be detailed and specific to be valuable. Bonus points for getting creative. Extra bonus points for surprising him.

Telling your partner you love her once a week is not enough. It's this continuous exchange of appreciation, this constant display of how you are both valuable to each other, that adds depth and strength to your relationship. It leaves no one wondering if they are important.

PRACTICE IN THE GOOD TIMES

It's an easy trap to only talk about feelings when something negative has happened. It's a mistake to expect your partner to understand your emotions or what's important to you—it's up to you to communicate that.

Don't wait until there are problems or until it is too late to practice good communication. As the old song goes, accentuate the positive.

Some people respond to verbal affirmation more than others, but it never hurts to say something appreciative and compliment your partner every day. It can be something small, but for it to be sincere and effective, it helps to provide details.

Don't use the same compliment repeatedly. If you find that you can't come up with more than one compliment to give, spend fifteen minutes alone and write down at least five things you appreciate about your partner. Keep your list somewhere easily accessible if you really need inspiration. The praise can cover anything, from their appearance to their behaviour to their own unique qualities. For example:

- "You look so handsome in that outfit [or out of it!]."

- "You've been very understanding of me lately, and I really appreciate it, darling."

- "I love your sense of humour."

This habit of noticing the good things about your partner is a real mood booster—for both of you!—as it promotes all the loved-up emotions that make your relationship work well. But it has to work both ways. Both of you must form this pattern.

(A popular book on this topic, *The Five Love Languages* by Dr. Gary Chapman, posits there are five love languages: Words of Affirmation, Acts of Service, Receiving Gifts, Quality Time, and Physical Touch. There's even a quiz people can take to learn the hierarchy of their own love languages, which helps people speak to their partners and loved ones in a way they will most understand. Learn more at [https://www.5lovelanguages.com].

SCHEDULE A REVIEW

Find some time when there are no particular issues needing attention, and use it to reflect on your relationship. It's best if the analysis happens in the cool light of day, perhaps over coffee, as opposed to during a dinner date or other social time.

I usually encourage couples to do this at least once a year and to see it as a useful study of the relationship. These reviews should cover practical things like finances, baby minding, and holidays, but there should also be time to discuss what works well emotionally and what needs some attention.

The benefit of making this conversation more business-like is it provides a structured and unemotional way of addressing issues and assessing how well our solutions are working. We use this intervention-like strategy in our work lives, but we can be slow to use it in marriages. However, if your relationship dynamic shies away from emotional outbursts or messy expressions of love, this approach is a fantastic way to get into the meat of your relationship without scaring anyone away.

Bottom line: it's a big mistake to assume your partnership will flourish all by itself, that love will be enough. It won't. You cannot assume that everything is fine if you do not ask, and a review is a very constructive way to adjust or reset your relationship.

So, find out what language resonates with your spouse and get talking.

VALUE DIFFERENCES AND PLAY TO YOUR STRENGTHS

You both bring something different to the success of your lives as individuals and as a couple—and valuing each person's contribution is crucial. Maybe one of you is good at planning, managing the finances, and arranging holidays, while the other is more gregarious, connecting more easily, making friends, and establishing a social network. These aspects bring different things to your lives, and all are important. Try to remember that. You need not be the same to find common ground—but you do need to be a unit, each of you bringing a complementary mixture of strengths and resources, where the whole is greater than the sum of the parts. This is how you can build a winning team.

Exercise Four:
How to Have a Difficult Conversation

Rationale

In close relationships, it's vital that partners resolve their differences and arguments in a gentle, clear, and positive way.

Method

1. **Rehearse what you want to say.** Write it down ahead of time if you think that will help.

2. **Focus only on the present issue.** Do not bring up the past.

3. **Speak first about what is going well** in your relationship. Express your love for your partner and let her know how important she is to you.

4. **Raise the issue**, but from the perspective of how it feels for you. State its impact on you and why you are asking for things to change.

5. **Listen to your partner's point of view.** Try to focus on understanding them rather than criticising. Frequently, couples get stuck right here and forget to make suggestions or plans for how to improve the situation.

6. **Suggest how you might go forward.** Positively embrace both perspectives. Make small changes first and then see how that works before pushing forward.

7. **Agree to review the issue at a set time.** You'll not only notice your progress, but also you'll begin to see that your difficulties can be sorted when you work together on a plan.

RESULT

Disagreements managed this way do not become destructive but instead stay focused on finding solutions to the issue at hand. Arguments can be a point of growth for you both as you begin to understand each other better and are more open to listening and cooperating.

CHAPTER FIVE:

HAVING FUN AND INTIMACY DESPITE IT ALL

“There's no fear when you're having fun.

—Will Thomas

What if, for some reason, being in lockdown is your partner's secret fantasy—and now she's pursuing you for sex? While you can't believe this is something you'd ever complain about (because you honestly do appreciate her enthusiasm and don't want to embarrass her or cause her to withdraw), you do want to make toast in your pyjamas without being fondled.

Or maybe sex is not the glue that holds the relationship together; it's nice when it happens, but it's not the main focus. And then one day your mate decides he wants to experiment with Viagra.

If this sounds like your secret nightmare, consider the following:

- Has something significant changed, and has this shift impacted your sex drive? Does it reflect a problem in your relationship? Do you feel unloved, unsupported, or bullied?

- If there's an age difference between you and your partner, that can be a factor, and so can menopause or age-related erectile dysfunction. If your wife consistently wanted more sex than you, then maybe you've always been trying to respond and keep up. But now it may be just too difficult.

- It's also possible that you're not sexually compatible, which is as significant as any other rapport in your relationship.

VARIATION AND SEX DRIVE

In a long-term relationship, you're bound to experience different levels of sex drive from time to time. Stress can have a range of effects on the libido as well. For some people, sex provides the adrenalin surge and hit of dopamine that stressed brains crave. Others find that their sex drive completely shuts down until they can regulate their emotions and find balance and control again.

Researchers at the US-based Kinsey Institute are studying how the COVID-19 pandemic is affecting people's sex lives and relationships. Most of the respondents say they're experiencing a decline in their sexual desire and behaviour.

HOW DO YOU RE-ESTABLISH INTIMACY?

If you haven't been intimate for a long while, taking the first step towards renewing your sexual connection will be hard. Just like diving into icy water, you've just got to squeeze up some courage and do it. Chances are your relationship has become largely transactional and that your focus has been too much on the business end of your life together.

When the earlier fires of passion have cooled, sometimes we need to be reminded of the obvious first step: to initiate physical intimacy, start with touch. Here are some additional steps to re-establishing physical connection:

1. As long as you have consent, begin by hugging and caressing your partner throughout the day. Do nothing that demands a response or immediate reciprocation, but rather use touch intended only to surprise her and make her feel good. Notice the results.

2. Agree to set aside time for sensual touching, but keep intercourse off the agenda. It takes away the pressure from the situation and allows you to focus on each other erotically.

3. Don't rush to the next stage; taking your time will allow all of your attention to stay in the moment.

4. Give yourself enough time to explore this stage and become comfortable with it.

5. The next stage only happens if the person who was more reticent about sex wants to progress. Allow them to make the call.

In my thirty-plus years as a therapist, I have seen time and time again that this is *the* method that works.

You've got to have fun

Spending every moment together and worrying about the world and this pandemic can certainly dampen your spirits, but this is when you need intimacy and fun the most.

In your pre-lockdown days, your life had a pattern: weekdays were about work, and weekends were for fun. But where's the enjoyment now? It's a challenge, obviously.

Before the pandemic, were you the one who organised activities every Saturday night, or did you let the weekends roll in without thought or plan? Did you connect with your girlfriends and keep in touch with friends and family? If you have always been a social person, you may find it easy to stay in touch, but that's not how it is for everyone.

Social connection is healthy for all of us; during this pandemic it will be more important than ever. Your mood, mental health, and your relationship will suffer without it. Our nervous system is designed to engage with others. When we're isolated, our emotions and behaviour can become erratic, and our bodies can experience physical pain. For some it can feel like a death sentence, and just the thought of isolation can cause panic.

While you may think you'll only benefit if you see people in person, meeting with your friends online will distract you from worries. It'll also help you hear how others are coping, which will give you a fresh perspective and make you feel less alone.

How to date when you're locked in 24/7

You must try to have pleasure despite the pandemic; however, the onus is on you to make it happen, and not just for you. Schedule enjoyable things for you to do as a couple. For example, every Friday night my husband and I meet our friends online for a virtual dinner party. We get dressed up for the occasion and cook a special meal. It really is the highlight of my week.

One couple I know of enjoys music from the '80s; they sometimes spend a few hours on a Friday or Saturday night playing videos from that era, loudly (and badly) singing along with them. Still another couple told me how they start the day with dancing in the kitchen to one of their favourite tunes. And, remember, just because we're cooped up in the house doesn't mean we don't have to dress up. A fresh shave and a splash of cologne, and some stockings and high heels and lipstick can do wonders for morale.

Fun and intimacy go together like ice cream and chocolate sauce. It's like insurance for your relationship—and it will get you through the bad times.

EXERCISE FIVE:
PRACTICE TOUCH AND ENGAGE THE SENSES

RATIONALE

It's easy to forget about touching when you're in a relationship. This is a shame because the "love hormone" oxytocin—which helps you feel more bonded and more forgiving of each other—releases when you hug, touch, or orgasm. Oxytocin also does nice things for the body, like making you feel less stressed and anxious.

METHOD

Experiment with engaging your senses of touch, sound, and smell:

- Collect five items that you will touch your partner with—for example, a feather, a brush, cotton wool or other material. Ask your partner to close their eyes—or, even better, wear a blindfold; have them guess the item being used. Ensure that both of you get a turn. Repeat the exercise again, but this time touch with your fingertips only.

- To play with sound, have one partner blindfolded while the other uses things to make sounds (for example, flick the teeth of a comb, or shake a bottle of peppercorns, or swoosh a carton of milk) which the blindfolded partner can guess at. Or perhaps play fragments of songs for a game of "name that tune."

- To engage the sense of smell, have one partner bring things to the blindfolded partner—a pat of butter, different spices, essential oils, some wine, some fresh-squeezed lemon juice.

RESULT

This exercise will make you more sensitive to touch, sound, and scent while having light-hearted physical contact—and you'll have fun guessing and competing with your mate.

CHAPTER SIX:

PARENTING THROUGH THE PANDEMIC

"When faced with the challenge, look for a way, not a way out.

—David L. Weatherford

Remember all the cute stuff you love about your children, like their darling chitter chatter? Now you're forced to listen to it *all day long*.

Or are you battling with your teenagers? It' so much fun trying to keep them safe against their will, isn't it? No, you can't *just* chill in the park, you tell them for the thirtieth time. No, Johnny CAN'T come *just* to hang out. No, your girlfriend can't quarantine with you alone in your room with the door shut.

Picking your battles

Parenting is always challenging, and in this pandemic period it's gotten even more intense. Gone are all the supports that have kept you feeling sane and relatively competent: no more day care, school, sports teams, or play dates. On top of all the other reality-flipping life changes, you are now one hundred percent responsible for your kids' entertainment, education, social development, and mental health. And you're also reminded daily that your success in all these areas will determine if they will ever find a job, healthy love, or the drive to move out on their own. No pressure!

If your child (no matter what their age) is arguing with you, pushing the boundaries, challenging your authority at every turn, well, that's a sign you must pick your battles wisely, only engaging when absolutely necessary. Hold your line and try to keep your cool because, if you don't, there's literally no escape.

Take screen time, for example. You've read all the literature about how developing brains must limit exposure to television and computer screens. That advice is now cancelled. Don't fight this battle too hard, but try to set some easy-to-maintain boundaries, like "You can watch all the TV you want after 4 p.m."

And here's another tip: In a calm moment, you can ask your partner to help handle these flashpoints with your children. Whoever has more patience could take the lead on the discussions. For example, if there's already tension between you and your daughter, why not let your spouse deal with her?

When you're still working

Not everyone is sitting at home with time on their hands—some people still have their jobs. And while you're lucky not to have your income interrupted, there are still some challenges to working at home. Here's how to face them:

- Keep office hours. They don't have to be the traditional nine to five, but they need to be regular. And it's even better if you can post them on your closed office door.

- At the office, you've got coffee and lunch breaks and time to socialise and build relationships with your co-workers. Your family members are your office mates now. Schedule breaks to make yourself available. Take a moment to chat to your children about the projects you're all working on. This will help them stay focused on their schoolwork and keep you connected.

- Treat your children like the unpaid assistants you always wanted and get them to bring you coffee. Kids want to be useful, and they're less likely to seek your attention at inappropriate times if they've got some helpful jobs to do.

- Keep your family posted about what you're working on and how things are progressing. If they know what's taking up your time, they're more likely to respect it.

- Stay professional, but don't get too strict about it. Now that everyone is being forced to work from home, we are redefining what professional looks like. Don't get too uptight if your kids interrupt your video conference. If you can, introduce them to the others on your call. You're a human being with lots of pulls on your attention. This is an opportunity to be honest about what those demands are and maybe get some leeway from your employer and colleagues.

When you're both working outside the home

This can be an incredibly difficult time for you as you're carrying all your normal responsibilities along with concerns about bringing the virus into your home. The only way this will work is to rally the troops. You can start by trying the following:

- If your children are over the age of four, involve them in meal preparation, housecleaning, and other chores. Tell them this is training for when they become independent or when they become roommates or partners. By giving your kids responsibilities, you're doing them a tremendous favour. Every person needs to feel useful and to know they have something valuable to contribute. I can tell you that being trusted with valuable tasks at a young age can do wonders for a child's confidence.

- It's well understood clinically that people will rise to the level of expectation you set for them, especially if you reward them for it. You could offer a way to earn an extra story at bedtime or other meaningful treats.

- Create a simple visual task list for everyone in the household, and have the kids involved in deciding what goes on the list. Encourage the whole family to participate in the creation of the list so they feel ownership; children who can't yet read or write can help decorate the task list while you read it to them so they feel like an important part of the process. If you'd like additional inspiration, do an online search on Pinterest for "family chore board ideas."

When only one of you is working outside the home

I don't know how front-line workers are being treated in your community, but in the home, that person should have elevated status during this pandemic. They're putting it all on the line for your family and managing the fallout from the public's stress and your own. For your mate to maintain their energy and health, they need to replenish at home where they feel safe and loved. How can you as the loving, supportive spouse help them at the end of a hard day?

It's vitally important to keep your partner's spirits up. If they know you appreciate and value their efforts, whatever happens in the outside world won't necessarily exact a high toll.

Before the feminist movement was prominent, women were schooled on how to greet their husbands when they came home from work. The advice given in every cookbook and magazine from the 1950s said that wives should don makeup and a pretty dress, make sure the house was clean, and lovingly embrace their husbands at his return to his castle. Furthermore, they were to greet him with a friendly hello (and a stiff drink) and avoid bothering him with complaints and problems for at least the first hour that he was home.

Sounds so archaic, doesn't it? But right now, during this difficult time, it's a great primer on how to lovingly support the spouse of any gender who has to leave the house every day for work.

When one of you is newly unemployed

It's always difficult to lose a job. Not only does it trigger uncertainty of when you will work again, but it can make you feel unwanted and unvalued. It's also not uncommon to have feelings of grief, betrayal, and anger. Many have a difficult time with job loss, as people often tie their identities and sense of purpose and belonging to their position. Here are a few suggestions for moving through this loss:

- Agree to a mourning period to allow for some grieving and sadness. During this time, the unemployed partner will not be peppered with advice or told to check out job postings. Instead, they will be fed and cared for.

- The mourning period needs an end date, and when that date comes the unemployed person may no longer mope or whine. There's too much to do! It may not be ideal to look for work during a global pandemic, but it is an excellent time to support their working spouse and kids. Get down to it—there's still washing up to do!

- Remember that once the economy moves again, opportunities will open up again, guaranteed. Now is a good time to prepare. Update your resume. Take an online training class. Work your network. Believe that on the other side of crisis lies opportunity.

When both of you have lost your jobs

Now it's more important than ever to treat each other with loving kindness. Together, you will get through this. To make this easier, try these tips:

- Give each other space to feel the emotions associated with this job loss. Recognise this period of recovery may not look the same for both of you. Make time to listen to each other. Allow some venting.

- If one of you feels the other sinking into a pit of despair, pull them out. Go for a walk. Bake some bread together. Try a new hobby. These are not normal times, and this was not a normal firing. The same rules do not apply. It's more important to keep your spirits up so you can see opportunities as they arrive and still have enough confidence to act on them.

- Dump all your negative thoughts and fears into a journal. It's easier to face them in writing, and it'll stop you from endlessly complaining to your spouse. Eventually, you can record things you're grateful for and things that are working well.

- Once you've written about your feelings for a while, create a strategy for your employment search. Map out the details of your assets and liabilities, and create action plans to move forward. Planning and knowing what specific behaviours you need to do every day will reduce anxiety levels substantially.

WHEN YOU'RE WORRIED ABOUT MONEY

You're in good company. Finances are a huge concern for individuals and governments around the globe right now. Half of the world's population is in lockdown at the time of writing this book, and governments everywhere are establishing systems to ease people's economic pressures.

Now is a good time to grab hold of your personal and household finances. It's also a perfect time to stop the clock—after all, you're not going out to restaurants and bars anymore, and you're not window shopping.

- Start today by hauling out that pile of unopened statements and bills. If you've been avoiding this, then you know you can't escape it. Put on some uplifting music or an interesting podcast or audiobook, get in the zone, and own it. Like ripping off a Band-aid, the fear loses its power once you face it.

- The more information you have, the more powerful you'll feel. Look over every bank statement and every account—just how much money do you have or owe? Create a spreadsheet or a list.

- Be brave and look three months down the road. What can you defer or cancel to give you a bit of breathing space right now? Call all your creditors and ask them for a grace period; it's entirely possible they will grant it to you.

- Once you fully understand your financial situation, start researching ways to improve it. Check with your financial institution to see if they have any resources to support you at this time.

Don't ignore these issues—the luxury of avoidance and postponement is no longer available. Your brain knows you're avoiding something important, and it will keep you anxious and awake at night until you deal with it. Use this time, when things are slow and when government and banks are offering assistance, to deal with your financial issues once and for all.

If you can face up to the truth of your situation and make new plans and resolutions for the future, then your relationship can be in better shape after the pandemic than before.

Exercise Six:
Get Better at Saying "No"

Rationale

You must be confident in saying no to others. If you submit to people's demands while ignoring your own needs and feelings, it can cause resentment and create other negative feelings within the relationship.

> How others respond to your boundaries is not your problem. Boundaries are for your protection, not to make others feel comfortable.
>
> —Emma Zeck

Method

Think about a current situation where you would like to say "no" but you are finding it difficult.

First, notice how the request affects your emotions by asking yourself the following:

- Do you feel obliged to meet the request? If so, why?

- Will you feel guilty or selfish if you say no?

- Is the person making the request causing you to feel this way, or are the feelings originating from inside you? Is it possible that it's not so much the request as it is *the way* it's being made?

- Write what makes you feel uncomfortable about saying "yes."

When you have decided that "no" is the answer:

- Acknowledge the request. Be specific about what they have asked; do not make presumptions—just repeat the request.

  "You asked if _______."

  "You'd like me to ______."

- Be clear and use the word "no."

  "I cannot ______."

  "I will not be able to _____."

  "I have to say no to _____."

- Acknowledge your discomfort, or guilt, or any other emotion if it helps you.

  "I'd like to do this for you, but I feel _____."

- "I feel guilty saying no because you probably think I have lots of time on my hands, but I don't."

- Remember that acknowledging your own feelings can help you feel stronger in the moment; you'll feel less stress when you take ownership of your own action.

- Practice saying "no" out loud. Listen to yourself and notice what feelings that brings up.

Result

Learning to say no effectively and without argument will help you to feel happier and more in control in all aspects of your life. It stops you submitting to other people's demands while ignoring your own needs and feelings. And it will allow you to have more honest, open relationships.

CHAPTER SEVEN:

SHOULD I STAY, OR SHOULD I GO?

> "And the day came when the risk to remain tight in a bud
> was more painful than the risk it took to blossom.
>
> —Anaïs Nin

When you fell in love, you thought it would be forever. Now you're wondering if forever will ever end.

What happens if you've done everything you can to turn this pandemic lockdown into a relationship oasis of sexy playfulness and emotional bonding, but it still hasn't worked? You can't stand your mate. Maybe you're looking at her right now, over the pages of this book, wondering how she could have blown it so badly. It could have been so easy to keep your love alive—all she needed to do was change, but she couldn't manage even that one simple thing.

COVID-19 is responsible for a lot of suffering and destruction across the globe, and after those going through illness and death, intimate relationships seem to have taken some of the hardest hits. In fact, just two months after lifting the lockdown in Wuhan, China, divorce applications increased by fifty-one percent.

Crises can break or make relationships; sometimes they shrink and wither, and at other times they expand and deepen. If you are only now realising that your partner will never change, and if that's a problem for you, don't beat yourself up about it. It's hard to get a clear sense of someone when you're just starting out. In the same way, often it takes a crisis to show you the depth of someone's character or to recognise you are not compatible.

But how do you know if the relationship you're in is reeling from the sucker punches of stress and instability or if it really is beyond fixing?

Most psychologists and relationship counsellors agree: if you answer yes to any of the following, it's a sign your relationships may be past saving.

- **You're afraid of your partner.** If you're unable to express yourself for fear of his reaction, or if you're walking on eggshells, worried about his unpredictable reactions, the relationship is no longer safe or authentic, and it's time to go.

- **One or both of you aren't willing to put in the effort.** If you won't seek any help, but you complain about her to anyone in earshot, you've got to ask yourself, "Why am I here?" When you're no longer inspired to give enough attention and care to meet her needs, then your relationship has fallen into a rut. This kind of relationship will diminish your self-worth and eat away at your confidence over time. That's too high a price for convenience, wouldn't you say?

- **The relationship feels toxic.** Have you forgotten what it feels like to enjoy his company? Do you feel better when you're alone? Do you brace yourself when you hear his footsteps approaching or when you sense he's about to open his mouth? This kind of relationship won't get better on its own. In fact, over time, it'll only get worse.

- **You're apathetic.** You no longer respect her or care enough even to fight, because really, what's the point? If you've lost passion, emotion, or even basic concern, this is a good indicator your relationship is past saving. If you can feel yourself starting down this road, get help as soon as you can because once you've reached the point of no return, there really isn't a way back.

- **The trust is gone.** If board games are no longer an option for evening entertainment because your spouse is a dirty cheat, relax and send him out to buy some toilet paper—board games aren't a deal-breaker. But if you've stopped sharing your plans for the future, and if you recoil at his tendency to tear down all your hopes and dreams, then emotional trust is no longer present, and it'll take a lot of effort to build it back up... if it can be rebuilt at all.

There's no fool-proof way to decide if it's time to pull the plug on your relationship; there are many factors to consider. For example, all marriages have high and low periods, and people grow apart and then come back together sometimes. The presence of young children complicate things and sometimes require compromises you'd never consider as a single person. While committed relationships can be a great place to work through your personal issues in order to grow and develop, they can also leave deep scars. Take care of yourself and be kind.

Even if you know that this relationship must end, the timing is important. Break-ups bring with them a type of grief, even though you might be glad to see the last of your ex. They've been part of your life, and you may miss that. You will weep for the relationship you had at the beginning and the relationship that might have been.

EXERCISE SEVEN:
LEARN TO SELF-DISCLOSE

RATIONALE

If you want to develop close relationships, you must be vulnerable and disclose things about yourself to another person. For couples, this has to be reciprocal.

(The topic of vulnerability has been more widely discussed in recent years as a result of researcher and storyteller Brené Brown's Ted Talks and books; she has excellent things to say about "the power of vulnerability," and a quick online search will offer you a wealth of results to explore.)

Some people find vulnerability very difficult. If you or your partner find it challenging, the following exercise can help you become more open with your partner—and vice versa.

METHOD

Ask each other the following questions as though it were an interview. Give your partner your full attention when they answer, and maintain eye contact with them throughout the exercise.

- Who would be your dream dinner guest?

- Who do you admire most in the world?

- What is the one thing you are most grateful for?

- If you could change one thing about your past, what would it be?

- If you could gain one quality or ability overnight, what would it be?

- What is the thing you have dreams about doing but have never done?

- What is your most precious memory?

- When did you last cry?

- Describe one of the most embarrassing moments you have experienced.

RESULT

This exercise encourages you to be vulnerable with each other, to share your memories and dreams that are precious to each of you. It will help you feel closer and to deepen your relationship.

CHAPTER EIGHT:

COMING OUT THE OTHER SIDE

> "Great occasions do not make heroes or cowards; they simply unveil them to our eyes. Silently and imperceptibly, as we wake or sleep, we grow strong or weak; and at last some crisis shows what we have become.
>
> —Brooke Foss Westcott

When you live through a crisis, such as serious illness, loss of a loved one, economic upheaval, wartime, or the COVID-19 pandemic, it forces an assessment of life's priorities—for example, what's most essential, what you want your life to look like, and who's important to you.

People often transform their lives after a crisis, finally making that radical change that they've been contemplating for a while. But the converse is also true: sometimes people find that what they were searching for—even if it was their "life's purpose"—has now lost its attraction and appeal.

In the same way that you'll view the world and your life differently after a crisis, you'll also gain fresh perspective on yourself. Maybe it'll help to think of yourself as the hero in your own personal movie.

While your partner may *think* they want you to have it all together from the very start, it will impress them more (and you too) if they see you gather strength and wisdom along the way and then put it all to good use by the end of your show. Next thing you know, they'll start referring to you as the next Liam Neeson or Charlize Theron. Finally!

This newfound strength and belief in yourself will enable you to overcome future challenges and also boost your confidence and self-esteem. (It might also help you land an Oscar.) The knowledge that you survived this difficult time has a big bright message attached—one that will trickle down to your unconscious mind: You were great. You managed. You kept your family going. You're strong and capable, so you need not feel so scared or anxious the next time a crisis arises.

Making it through the other side of the crisis also means you'll have a much clearer idea of how the two of you operate as a couple.

Here's a list of questions that will help you reflect on your experience and create an accurate account of how things have changed. Taking the time to reflect on the experience now will help you both to have greater clarity about what works well for you as a couple and what doesn't.

When answering these questions, try to provide as much detail as possible.

1. Do you love and value each other now as much as or more than before the crisis? Why?

2. How did you work through this crisis as a couple? Were you able to be a team, or were you two individuals struggling against each other?

3. What did you bicker about? Did you resolve those arguments and understand each other better afterward?

4. Did you work together to create a healthy home life during the crisis?

5. Did you support each other even on the most difficult of days, or did you find your partner too needy and negative?

Use this knowledge to create a strategy for how you'll approach life's next crisis. Notice what you did well and how you could improve on that. Where did you screw up? What can you do to prevent that from happening again?

What you learn through this time will help you for all the days of your life and every crisis that you meet. Because no one gets through life without a number of crises.

Exercise Eight:
Acknowledge Your Strengths

RATIONALE

It's important to recognise your own skills and strengths and to see how they have helped you to come through crisis and to accomplish different things in your life.

METHOD

Step 1: Recall a time that you found extremely stressful and whose onset was a surprise to you.

This could be a death, illness, or an accident, for example. Give yourself a full five minutes to think back on that event. Remember your earliest fears—how you felt right at the beginning of it. Then use your journal to write your answers to the following questions:

What were you mostly concerned about at the time?

- I thought...

- I feared...

- I worried...

Step 2: We often fear the worst, so it's important to check out what really happened. Because the reality can be very different.

- Which of these fears materialised?

- What really happened?

- How did things work out?

- Would you have the same fears now if the same situation was before you?

- What have you learnt about approaching a crisis from that event?

- What are the four most important things that you will try to remember for a future crisis like this one?

Step 3: Write a short note to your younger self. Tell her how to best manage that stressful situation now that you have learnt how to survive it.

- How would you advise her to soothe her fears?

- What do you think she could have done differently that might have helped?

- What soothing statement would you have for her now? What could you say to her that would help her face the situation with less fear and less concern?

Result

You have identified some skills that helped you through this period, and you've noted what lessons you have learnt and what skills you used. Hopefully, you can now see how much better prepared you are to face similar events in the near and distant future.

DEEPER ISSUES

"Through each crisis in life, with acceptance and hope, in a single defining moment, I finally got the courage to do things differently.

—Sharon E. Rainey

In the previous chapters, we've looked at how a crisis (in particular a lockdown) can affect your romantic relationship, and we've explored ways to strengthen your relationship during difficult times.

Some couples, however, have bigger, deeper issues that can quickly intensify when under the increased pressure of a lockdown or pandemic. In the next chapters we'll address the more common of these, and consider how to approach them during a crisis.

Chapter Nine:

Living With an Alcoholic

> "Learn to face things as they come with calm deliberation. We may not be able to control events, but we can control our attitudes towards them.
>
> —Al-Anon

Your partner has been drinking more than you're comfortable with. You've already had that awkward conversation. You've pleaded, even begged, for her to reduce her intake. You pointed out the damage it was doing to your lives, finances, and relationships. But nothing has changed, or maybe it did temporarily but just for a little while. Now you're on week three of a lockdown, and you can see that the problem is only getting worse.

She's not just having a few too many drinks while socialising with friends—she's undeniably an alcoholic.

If you're home with children, you'll probably want to maintain some normality for them while your partner drinks herself into an alcoholic slumber every night. You'll feel alone and, in truth, it would be easier if you were alone. Because now if you mention her drinking in any way it ends up in a blowout which is upsetting for you and the children. And it's not like you can just get up and leave, right?

But how you'd approach this issue during a crisis differs from more normal times. Even though you now recognise the problem for what it is, it's not imperative that you take action immediately. You'll need energy to manage just being at home in lockdown and distanced from other valuable supports.

Here's my advice on how you can survive this time with your alcoholic spouse, to lower your stress and keep your own mental health intact:

- **Shift your focus to yourself and your children** (if you have any). Stop paying attention to her drinking and ignore it in every way that you can.

- **Ask for practical help from your mate** and involve her in the plans for the day—shopping, gardening, or chores, for example. Recognise that she may not be capable or willing to take part, but the conversation you'll have about planning will at least prevent a hostile silence from building.

- **Don't wear the blame** when someone else chooses to drink. A person dependent on alcohol needs reasons to drink and will find them in the surrounding environment. They may say that someone is always nagging them, or that they need a break, or that they simply deserve it. These are good rationales in their mind. So, don't give them a reason to feel justified for excessive drinking—in other words, don't nag or argue. Save your energy and let her drink.

- **Avoid confrontation.** You've asked for improvements in your spouse's drinking habits, but it's not your job to remind her one hundred times that this is what you want. Just let that conversation rest.

- **Stop trying to fix it.** This is her problem. She's addicted, not you. She is responsible for her life, her health, and the damage that his drinking causes to others—and that includes you. It isn't up to you to make things right.

- **Address it later.** Decide that you can address this problem when you have the time and energy to do so, most likely after lockdown.

- **Research the facts.** Prepare for the time when you will address the problem by arming yourself with the facts. Research online for signs, symptoms, supports and treatment. Look specifically for the support and courses available for partners of alcoholics. Many of my clients find these sites very comforting as they realise they are not alone and that there are millions worldwide working through the same issue.

- **Get professional help** to discuss the problem and to establish when and how you will address your partner's alcoholism in the long term. You may wish to do an online search for Al-Anon, a "worldwide fellowship that offers a programme of recovery for the families and friends of alcoholics, whether or not the alcoholic recognises the existence of a drinking problem or seeks help."

- **Mind yourself.** Taking good care of yourself is vitally important not only for your own health but, if there are children, then at least one parent must function well. Eat well, exercise, and connect with your own friends if possible.

- **Switch off from the problem.** It's essential that you give yourself time when you are not thinking about your partner's drinking, the future, and how everything will work out. While inevitably it will worry you, you must actively distract your mind from this problem for some period. If you can, force yourself to begin something that demands you focus as it will allow you to switch off the worry and allow room for you to build perspective.

When lockdown is over and some normality has returned to your life, then address the issue fully. With the help of your online research and some professional support, you can intervene effectively and get your partner into treatment for her alcoholism.

I cannot overstate this: to be strong enough to manage this very stressful time, you must not underestimate the importance of minding your own health and well-being as a top priority.

In my experience, partners often give too much of themselves trying to fix the problem that belongs to someone else. I don't want that to be you!

Chapter Ten:

When You Don't Trust Your Mate

> "If you love them trust them. If you don't trust them, what are you doing with them?
>
> —Charles Orlando

Now that you're in lockdown, you're in an ideal position to eavesdrop on every conversation that your partner has. Suddenly, you're privy to parts of their lives that you never knew existed. Who's Sue? How come you've never mentioned her? And you're part of her knitting group? What? You know how to knit?

While you don't have to tell your spouse every little part of your day, there is an expectation that you will share most of it. The discovery that one of you hasn't been doing that can bring up the issue of trust.

Your relationship will only grow and strengthen if you trust each other.

Trust is the foundation that allows you to deepen your emotional and sexual connection and to build a relationship for the long term. But what if you don't trust your partner? Is it that they are untrustworthy, or is it more about you and your issues?

Ask yourself:

- Do you have a good reason for distrusting your mate?

- Is this lack of trust because of something they actually did, or is it something that you feared could happen?

- Have you found it difficult to trust in previous relationships?

Trust issues can stem from childhood or another relationship. If you've experienced serious disappointment, or emotional or sexual abuse of any kind, then you may find it difficult to trust.

Especially if you've been hurt as a child, your unconscious self will act like a security guard, always protecting your emotions, checking and distancing you from anyone who can harm (or love) you.

This protective mechanism is great when danger is present, but it can damage a relationship that's trying to grow. Not only is it distressing for you, it's also painful for your spouse, especially if she's done nothing wrong.

If you want to build a loving and trusting relationship with your spouse, try these four steps.

- **Acknowledge your feelings.** Think back to the pain and disappointment that you've experienced in the past and accept that it happened and that it's over. Without acknowledgement, this feeling will continue to impact your behaviour.

- **Work through your emotions.** Convey that emotion in a way that feels appropriate. For example, you could write a letter to the one who hurt you (but you don't have to give it to them or post it). Just getting in touch with your feelings and giving them expression will help you to work through them.

- **See your past from your present.** Try to look at the difference between your current and past situations. Recognise that your lover is not the person who disappointed you before. Notice how you've changed and how much stronger you are now.

- **Share your feelings with your partner.** Although it's your responsibility to sort out your personal business, telling your spouse what's going on and asking for their understanding will help build the trust between you.

Seek professional help if you're having difficulty at any part in this process.

CHAPTER ELEVEN:

INFIDELITY REARS ITS UGLY HEAD

“Every affair will redefine a relationship, and every relationship will determine what the legacy of the affair will be.
—Esther Perel

Yesterday, when you were on a video call with your spouse, the call was interrupted by a text from Sarah. Yes, that same Sarah that he was flirting with all of last year—and you're pretty sure they slept together. You thought that after all that counselling and fun times you and he have had together, Sarah was out of your life for good. Obviously you're wrong about that, but you're also locked down with this man. How in the world are you going to handle this?

Sexual infidelity is the biggest threat to a relationship and is often the reason that couples break up. But others work through this volatile time, exploring what happened and why, and then finding a new path forward.

If it was a dalliance at the Christmas office party that "just got out of hand," that's one thing. The affair that's been ongoing for years and denied despite all of your doubts is quite another.

Some things are easier to forgive; others you cannot.

Now that you know he's been in touch with Sarah again, you're mad as hell. You've packed his bags, and now you're contemplating taking a hammer to his model car collection. While it may feel great, and you're entitled to your anger, it's not the best way to respond.

I've seen many marriages and relationships saved because couples responded differently.

Here is an alternative approach to sending him packing:

- **Resist demonising.** Try to remember that the person you love is still there, even if he has hurt you.

- **Don't tell everyone.** While it may be oh-so-tempting to tell everyone what a bastard he has been, try to restrain yourself. Instead of dealing with their reactions, take the time to become clear about what you want to happen next.

- **Look for the reasons.** Try to discover what transpired and why. Understanding why the breach happened will undoubtedly be the most important factor in whether you as a couple can go forward. It may have been a distance that developed between you because one of you was absorbed by work, stress, or illness. Or maybe the wandering spouse was more susceptible to flattery and the validation and confidence boost that it provided.

- **Intervene early.** If you've decided you want to save your relationship, and the affair is still in its early stage (when the passion is at its highest), ask that they pause everything while the two of you work things out.

- **Appeal to the third party.** If you really want to save your marriage or long-term relationship, it's perfectly reasonable to go to the other woman or man and ask them to back off. Tell them you and your partner need time and space to work out your issues. Don't make this request vindictively or with blame. Simply explain in a very human way that you love each other and need some time to address your problems. In all my time as a therapist, I have never seen the "other" woman or man resist this appeal.

Remember, many people recover successfully from infidelity and build stronger and even more honest relationships afterwards. But that healing and rebuilding can only happen when there is truth and a love worth fighting for—and you must ask yourself if this relationship is worth it.

CHAPTER TWELVE:

WHEN THERE'S A POWER IMBALANCE

> "Abuse is the weakest expression of strength. It is weakness to destroy what you ought to protect, build, and make better.
> —Kingsley Opuwari Manuel

Has your partner always been protective of you, shielding you from others who he feels will hurt you or are bad for you? At first it may have felt like a compliment. But now you're beginning to wonder as now he's finding fault with your friends and family—even your mum!

You've tried to have the conversation with him, but it always ends up in a frightening argument, so you've continually backed down. And now here you are in lockdown with this man and these doubts.

A healthy relationship will never require you to sacrifice your friends, your dreams, or your dignity.

This, obviously, is not a good situation to be in.

Abuse of power in a relationship is like a weed: it takes over and damages everything. What begins as small signs of control often ends up in physical abuse. This is especially true if there's a confrontation or the abuser feels that they are losing control of you.

If you find yourself in this situation or you're feeling scared, you must pay attention to what your fear is telling you. When your friends tell you they're worried about you, hear them. Listen to your mum when she says she misses you.

If you are frightened, you must leave as soon as soon as possible. Remember that there are supports to help you leave.

But if you're not quite at the fear point, and since you're in lockdown, then this is not the ideal time for a confrontation. Above all else you must stay safe, stay calm, and create a strategy that will let you exit safely.

It's important that you know that any abuse of power in relationships builds over time and will deteriorate into more serious abuses.

Learn what advice and support is available to you. Consider talking to someone outside of your family; seek a professional familiar with these sorts of issues and how they may affect you, and who can guide your actions.

A great relationship is about two things: first, appreciating similarities, and second, respecting differences.

Healthy relationships have a smooth continuous sharing of power from one person to the other. Less healthy ones have a fight for dominance that brings about resentment and hurt over time, damaging or killing the relationship.

Think of it like a waltz, with the smooth shifting of weight between the two of you. And like a dance, it needs to be an effortless, easy movement—no tugging, pushing, fighting, or straining for control. It's the harmony between the two of you that makes the relationship work.

When things go wrong, it's often because there's a struggle for power. Understanding how that may have come about is essential both for the relationship and your own health.

This dynamic isn't always obvious at the outset, nor maybe for a while. So, don't feel bad thinking you should have seen it. Thousands of people miss it just like you did.

A few rules to keep in mind:

- Remember that you are in a relationship because you want to be—you're always free to leave. At any given moment you have the power to say, "This is not how the story is going to end."

- You should feel better in a relationship than when you are away from that person. If this isn't true for you, then why are you there?

- It's essential to have an emotional and sexual connection with your partner. Don't confuse this, however, as a deep bond or love if you are being controlled or abused in any manner.

- Beware of "gaslighting," a type of systematic psychological manipulation. The term comes from the 1938 stage play "Gas Light" where the husband slowly dims the home's gas lights over time. When his wife notices the lights are getting progressively dimmer, the husband says she's imagining things and makes her doubt her own perceptions and sanity. If your partner manipulates you into believing that you're wrong about something when you know that you aren't, then he is "gaslighting" you.

- If you feel fearful of your partner and of how they will react to you if you raise an issue of concern, this is the time to reach out. Please do not hesitate to call your local emergency services if there is domestic abuse. At any time, even in the midst of a global pandemic, there is help available to you.

CHAPTER THIRTEEN:

WHEN YOUR PARTNER HAS A MENTAL HEALTH ISSUE

> "Taking care of yourself doesn't mean me first—it means me too.
>
> —L.R. Knost

The limitations of lockdown and physical distancing can intensify the difficulties around mental health issues, not only for the individual themselves but for partners and family.

In addition to all the complexities of diagnosis and living with someone with a mental health issue, you also may feel that you have no support.

Even though you're in lockdown, you don't have to handle this problem alone:

- Professional help is very much available to you via online sessions. It's important to access these for advice on how to manage a situation or for direct intervention with the individual themselves.

- If your partner is displaying behaviours or mood changes that are new and different to what you've seen before, then your concerns may be well founded.

- If your mate has already received a diagnosis, then you already know which issues exacerbate their mental health, and you are likely confident in managing this. However, you're probably not prepared for how the added stress of a crisis may have escalated their behaviour. Find yourself personal or professional support to help you at this critical time.

- The doctor may prescribe medication to help stabilise the situation. Know that some medications, such as tranquillizers have an immediate effect, but others such as antidepressants take several weeks to have a full effect.

THINGS TO KEEP IN MIND WHEN YOU'RE IN A LOCKDOWN

The usual principles of self-care apply, except that they become more important at this time:

- Within the household you will need to create space for yourself, a time when you are not interacting with your partner or listening to their woes.

- Encourage structure and exercise. While your partner may not find the motivation to do these things, you must do them for yourself.

- Ask family and friends for support by keeping in contact with your partner.

CONCLUSION

The emergence of COVID-19 reminds us just how much of our lives can change in an instant. Now that we're a number of months into this pandemic, we've been through many different stages of adjustment. Such adjustment is exhausting and, if we're honest, even a little frightening.

But look how you've managed, and continue to manage, personally and as a couple. See how you've strengthened and grown. You've learned to keep an eye on what brought you together, and you're finding ways to quickly address the bugbear issues.

Having good habits in relationships is every bit as important as any other aspect of your life. You must communicate lovingly, remember the marvellous stuff, stay grateful, be confident in saying no, be assertive, and above all else expect a life together that is filled with love, fun, and mutual respect.

You'll meet other crises as a couple, but the positive habits and attitude that you've cultivated make you far more ready to deal with whatever comes your way.

ACKNOWLEDGEMENTS

Thank you to my Canadian editor and writing coach, Maria Lironi, for patiently guiding me through the entire process of writing this, my first book. It's almost as if we've been in lockdown together while writing this book, albeit on different continents; it has been a special exchange of two women's life experiences.

Thanks as well to my friend Grace Gerry, who introduced me to Maria and helped me realise that I could do this; to Maia Gibb and Renée Layberry for their editorial support; to the late Mel Calman, and his daughter Claire, for generously giving me permission to use his drawings in my book.

Finally, to my husband Liam Scott, who supports me in every step I take in life, no matter the direction. His first gift to me was Mel Calman's book, *But It's My Turn to Leave You . . .* which has thankfully never come to pass.

About the Author

Stephanie Regan is a clinical psychotherapist with more than thirty years of clinical experience and is a frequent contributor on Irish radio, television, and print. She is a graduate of University College Dublin, with a M.Sc. in Clinical Psychotherapy. Her other studies include Mathematics, Economics, and Social Work, also at UCD. For more information, please visit her website at [https://stephanieregan.ie].